A is for... Audré

Shevonica M Howell
Illustrated by: Farrah Prince

To order additional copies of this book, contact:
Xlibris
844-714-8691
www.Xlibris.com
Orders@Xlibris.com

ISBN: Softcover   978-1-6641-6522-9
         EBook   978-1-6641-6521-2

Print information available on the last page

Rev. date: 04/28/2021

This book was made especially
for Audre' R. Caldwell

WE LOVE YOU

is for

Audre'

is for

Brothers

C

is for

Cupcakes

D

is for

Daddy

is for

F

is for

Flowers

is for

Granny

H

is for

Happy

I

is for

Ice Cream

J

is for

Jacksonville

is for

L is for **Love**

M

is for

Mommy

N

is for

Nana

O

is for

Oranges

is for

PaPa

is for

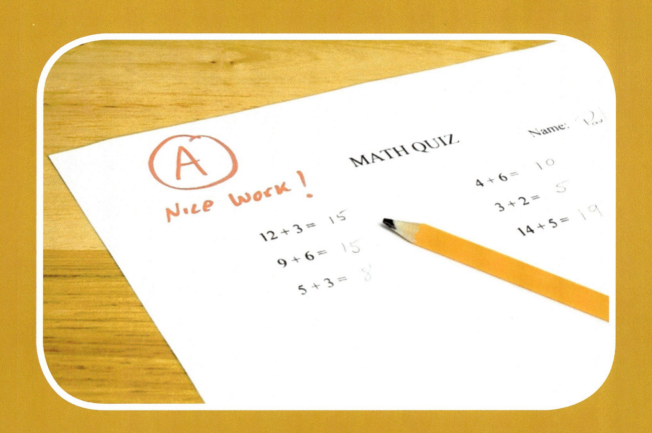

R

is for

Reading

S

is for

School

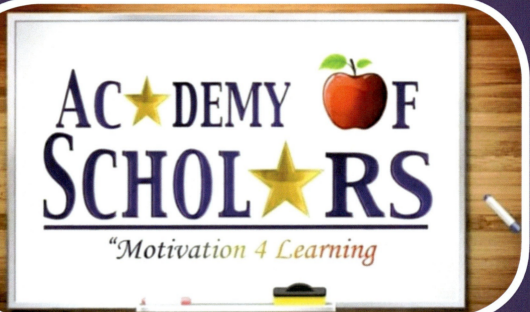

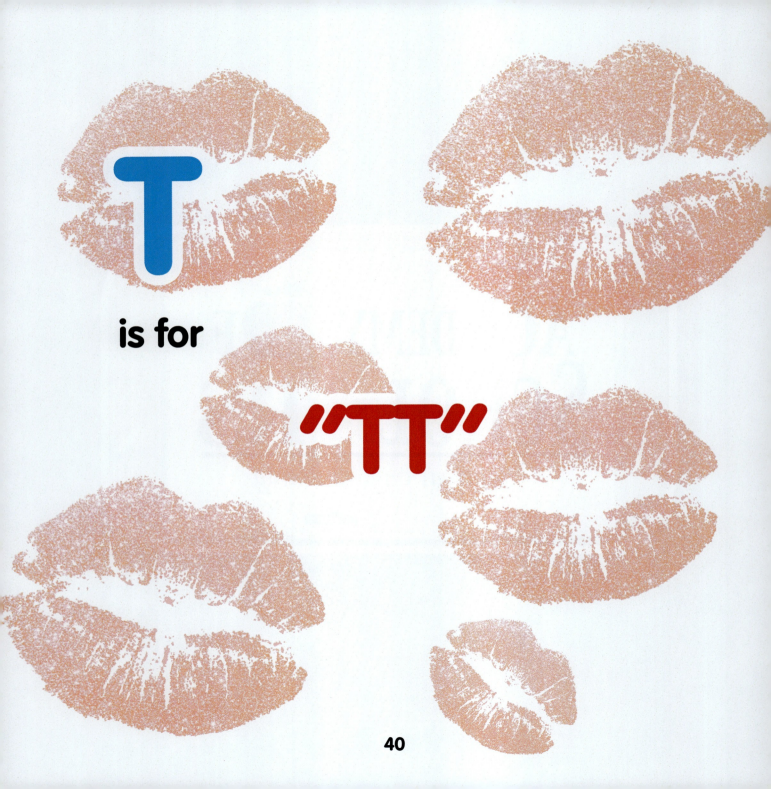

T is for **"TT"**

is for

Uncle and Unforgettable

V is for

Vowels

is for

Watermelon

is for

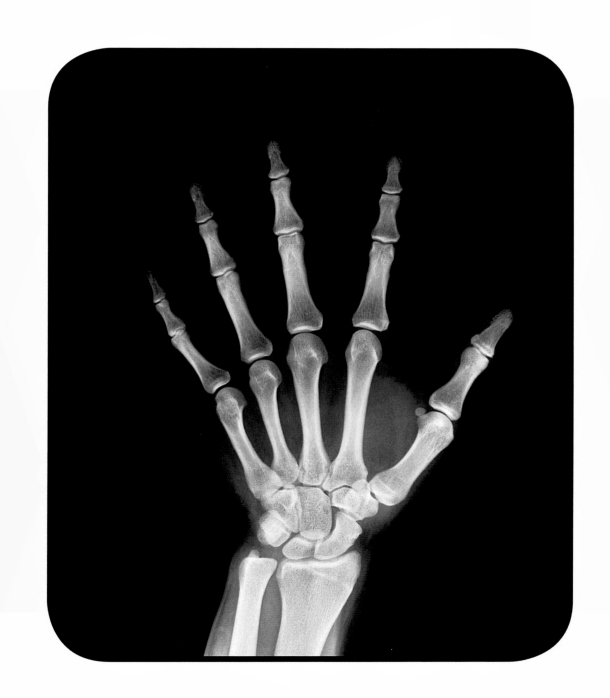

Y is for

Yellow

Z

is for

WELCOME TO THE ZOO

SIGHT WORDS

brothers
cupcakes
Daddy
eight
flowers
Granny
happy
ice cream
Jacksonville
kite
love

Mommy
Nana
oranges
PaPa
quiz
reading
school
Uncle
UNFORGETTABLE
vowels
watermelon
x-ray
yellow
zoo

GLOSSARY

Audre'	a smart, pretty, happy girl
brothers	funny, handsome, smart boys with a sister
cookies	small, sweet, flat cakes that are normally round
cupcakes	sweet, miniature cakes
Daddy	a handsome Father that love and care for his children
eight	the number after seven but before nine
flower	the pretty, colorful part of a plant
Granny	a loving Grandmother that spoils her kids and grandkids
happy	to be filled with joy
ice cream	a sweet, frozen food made of cream or milk
Jacksonville	a city in Duval County, Florida
kite	a fun toy that can fly
love	to like very much
Mommy	a pretty Mother that love and care for her children
Nana	a special name for an Aunt that love and care for everyone
oranges	a sweet, round fruit with an orange color
PaPa	a special name for a funny, helpful Grandfather
quiz	a short test or exam
reading	to pronounce, read and understand words
school	a place to make friends and learn

"TT"	a special name for a pretty Auntie that loves her nieces and nephews
Uncle	a funny, handsome man that loves his nieces and nephews
Unforgettable	uncapable of being forgotten; memorable
vowels	are the letters: A, E, I, O, U and sometimes Y
watermelon	an oval-shaped, green fruit that is normally red inside with seeds
x-ray	a tool that shows the bones and inside of a body
yellow	a color in the rainbow
zoo	a fun place with rides and animals

GLOSSARY ACTIVITY

Use the glossary to answer the questions below.

1. What is a quiz? _____

2. The letters, A, E, I, O, U, and sometimes Y are called _____

3. _____ is a sweet, frozen food made of cream or milk.

4. Define school. _____

5. What is a zoo? _____

6. A tool that shows the bones and inside of a body is called an _____

7. Watermelon is a(n) _____

8. _____ is a city in Duval County, Florida.

9. Define love. _____

Word Search

cupcakes   eight   flowers   happy

ice cream   Jacksonville   kite   love

oranges   quiz

g	i	z	s	q	f	c	q	u	i	z	n
w	l	v	e	b	l	g	e	h	k	y	s
j	a	c	k	s	o	n	v	i	l	l	e
y	p	p	a	h	w	q	t	m	r	i	g
f	l	n	c	y	e	e	y	o	g	x	n
m	o	y	p	h	r	w	r	h	e	s	a
k	v	j	u	m	s	z	t	l	d	z	r
o	e	i	c	e	c	r	e	a	m	k	o

READING ACTIVITY

1. Who is the Author of this book?

_____

2. Who illustrated this book?

_____

3. What is the title of this book?

_____

4. What was this book about?

_____

5. Which letters were your favorite letters?

_____

6. If you wrote a book, what would you name it?

_____

7. Did you enjoy this book? Circle YES or NO.

_____

8. If you enjoyed this book, list two reasons why you enjoyed it.

_____

_____

_____

9. If you did not enjoy this book, list two reasons why you did not enjoy it.

_____

_____

10. Write about a family member or friend that is UNFORGETTABLE to you.

_____

_____

_____

Shevonica M. Howell is the Founder & CEO of Academy of Scholars, Inc., a private school in Jacksonville, FL. She is also the author of The "YOU TEACH IT" Math Study Guide, A Play with Words Word Search Puzzle Book, and three nonfiction books. She has a son, daughter, and two grandkids. ShevonicaMHowell@gmail.com

Farrah Milan Prince is a self-taught Artist and college student from Jacksonville, Florida. Ms. Prince is also the illustrator of What's in a Name. Ms. Prince is a passionate Artist that has always had a love for drawing and painting. Ms. Prince remains humbled and grateful to her family for believing in her craft and for blessing her with their unwavering love and support. FarrahMilan06@gmail.com

Printed in the United States
by Baker & Taylor Publisher Services

Xlibris

The Adventures of Abby and the Seahorse

Go to Texas

B.I PHILLIPS